I0177755

# *Also by Andre Bagoo*

## *POETRY:*

*Trick Vessels,* (Shearsman, 2012)

*BURN,* (Shearsman, 2015)

*Pitch Lake,* (Peepal Tree, 2017)

*The City of Dreadful Night,* (Hesterglock, 2018).

## *ESSAYS:*

*The Undiscovered Country,* (Peepal Tree, 2020)

# WRITING THROUGH SIDDHARTHA

*Bagoo*

Scan QR Code for an audio recording of *Writing through Siddhartha* by the author Andre Bagoo.

ISBN: 978-1-913642-80-8

The author/s has asserted their right to be identified as the author of this Work in accordance with the Copyright, Designs and Patents Act 1988

Cover designed by Aaron Kent

Edited and typeset by Aaron Kent

Broken Sleep Books (2021): Talgarreg, Wales

# *Contents*

how? how you said
  —John Cage, *Writing through Finnegans Wake*

the words came flowing to him
  —Herman Hesse, *Siddhartha*

# Writing through Siddhartha

Andre Bagoo

# Afterwards

a long detour
a long look
a long meditative recitation
a long path
a long pause
a long sequence
a long silence had occurred
a long time
a long time after midnight
a long time afterwards
a long time ago
a long time had yearned
a longing

a bird or
a bird's appetite
a bit
a bit denser every day
a bit different
a bit heavier
a bit murkier every month
a bit silly yes
a bit strange
a bizarre
a blessing
a blossom
a boat
a bottomless pit

thus without reason
time
Time is
time she
times
times but
Timid
timidly fled
timidness
tiny
tired
tired mouth
tiredness
tiredness came over Siddhartha
tiredness has overwhelmed me

# Writing for the Second Time through *Siddhartha*

his ardent will
his arms
his arms folded
his arms were hanging down
his beard
his breath
his business-deals
his chest
his companion
his counterpart
his course
his dormant spirit suddenly woke up
his entire body like the lukewarm
his entire long sleep had been nothing but
his eyes
his eyes became motionless
his eyes fixed
his eyes were fixed on
his eyes were rigidly focused towards
his eyes were starting
his face
his farewell
his fate
his father
his father appeared
his father felt
his father had said
his father's son
his fear
his fears flowed
his feet
his finger closed her eyelids
his forehead
his friend
his futile fight against them
his future is already
his gestures
His glance turned
his goal
His goal attracts him

his greeting
his guest while asking
his heart
his heart felt cold
his heart full
his heart his own life
his high calling
his landlord's business
his liberated
his life had been
His life had indeed been strange
his mind
his mind becoming one with
his mockery had become more tired
his mother sang
his mouth twitched
his own image
his own knowledge
his own search
his own search able
his own suffering
his pain will be
his path
his path had passed through life
his power
his quietly dangling hand
his quietly lowered glance
his respect
his self
his self had flown into the oneness
his self had retreated
His senses
his senses had become alive
his servant
his shadow
his shoulders
his skin
his small
his smile
his smile became more similar

his smile shone golden
his solid staff
his son
his son appeared
his soul
his soul die
his soul sent after the Brahman as
his spear-carrier
his spell
his suffering was
his superiority had become more
his teachings
his teachings be strange
his teachings sound foolish
his thighs
his walk
his way against her
his will was
His wound blossomed
his yellow cloak

# Writing for the Third Time through *Siddhartha*

Siddhartha also felt desire
Siddhartha also remembered everything
Siddhartha answered
Siddhartha asked his host
Siddhartha ate his own bread
Siddhartha awakened
Siddhartha began
Siddhartha bent down
Siddhartha bid his farewell
Siddhartha bowed with
Siddhartha can wait calmly
Siddhartha collapsed
Siddhartha continued
Siddhartha could
Siddhartha did
Siddhartha does
Siddhartha emerged
Siddhartha entered the chamber
Siddhartha even doubted
Siddhartha exclaimed
Siddhartha exposed himself
Siddhartha felt
Siddhartha felt his blood heating up
Siddhartha felt more
Siddhartha ferried across
Siddhartha found himself being dragged away
Siddhartha gave him
Siddhartha gave his garments
Siddhartha got
Siddhartha had
Siddhartha had also been hearing
Siddhartha had always watched
Siddhartha had assumed
Siddhartha had been partaking
Siddhartha had gotten into
Siddhartha had intended to
Siddhartha had learned
Siddhartha had lived the life
Siddhartha had spent the night
Siddhartha had started

Siddhartha had venerated
Siddhartha had woken up
Siddhartha hadn't
Siddhartha hardly felt
Siddhartha has always obeyed his father
Siddhartha has come
Siddhartha has set harder goals for
Siddhartha himself
Siddhartha informed the oldest one
Siddhartha is putting me on
Siddhartha kindly spoke
Siddhartha knew
Siddhartha knew many venerable Brahmans
Siddhartha laughed
Siddhartha lay down
Siddhartha learned
Siddhartha learned something new
Siddhartha left his garden
Siddhartha listened
Siddhartha looked
Siddhartha looked into his friendly face
Siddhartha looked into the water
Siddhartha looked over
Siddhartha lost his
Siddhartha made
Siddhartha never listened
Siddhartha nodded
Siddhartha once again forced his mother
Siddhartha only ate once
Siddhartha opened his eyes
Siddhartha placed his hand
Siddhartha pondered
Siddhartha practised
Siddhartha reached the large river
Siddhartha realised
Siddhartha recognised him
Siddhartha remained standing there
Siddhartha repeated murmuring the verse
Siddhartha right here
Siddhartha rose

Siddhartha said
Siddhartha said nothing
Siddhartha said quietly
Siddhartha said tiredly
Siddhartha sat
Siddhartha sat down next
Siddhartha sat upright
Siddhartha saw
Siddhartha saw a
Siddhartha saw him
Siddhartha saw how beautiful she was
Siddhartha saw it
Siddhartha smiled
Siddhartha spared him
Siddhartha spoke
Siddhartha spoke in
Siddhartha spoke one day while begging
Siddhartha spoke sadly
Siddhartha spoke to
Siddhartha stayed
Siddhartha stood
Siddhartha stood silently
Siddhartha stopped
Siddhartha stopped fighting his fate
Siddhartha stopped once again
Siddhartha straightened up
Siddhartha succeeded
Siddhartha suddenly had
Siddhartha surpassed him
Siddhartha thanked
Siddhartha thanked her
Siddhartha the greedy could also die
Siddhartha the rich man
Siddhartha thought
Siddhartha thought about his situation
Siddhartha took
Siddhartha understood
Siddhartha waited
Siddhartha walked through the forest
Siddhartha walked through the lanes

Siddhartha watched him leave
Siddhartha watched him leaving
Siddhartha watched the leaving monk
Siddhartha wavered
Siddhartha went
Siddhartha will do what his father will tell him
Siddhartha will go
Siddhartha will return

Siddhartha's ear
Siddhartha's eyes
Siddhartha's eyes read the suffering
Siddhartha's face
Siddhartha's hand
Siddhartha's interest
Siddhartha's previous births were
Siddhartha's shoulder
Siddhartha's soul slipped inside the body

# Writing for the Fourth Time
## through *Siddhartha*

flocked
flowed
flowers
flowing
fly
foamed
folded
follow

saw agni he saw all
saw him standing
saw his body full
saw his head full
saw his own face lying
saw his steps full of
saw Kamala's
saw Krishna
saw no images any more
saw no joy any
saw no trembling
saw Siddhartha standing
saw the
saw the reflection of
saw the servants
saw the young man standing there
saw them achieving infinitely much
saw them complaining about pain
saw them suffering

she admitted
she asked
she became aware
she beckoned him
she called out
she exchanged humorous
she gazed after it
she had
she had aroused him
she had felt
she had gone
she had retired
she had said
she had seen the other one
she lay
she lifted her head
she looked
she loved his voice
she loved the look from
she opened the door

Govinda also realized
Govinda answered
Govinda bowed
Govinda exclaimed loudly
Govinda had aged
Govinda had become a
Govinda had said
Govinda has heard the teachings
Govinda knew
Govinda listened
Govinda listened silently
Govinda looked
Govinda made the gesture
Govinda realized
Govinda said
Govinda saw
Govinda spoke
Govinda spoke one day
Govinda stared
Govinda stayed the night
Govinda stopped
Govinda turned pale
Govinda twenty paces away
Govinda urged his friend
Govinda used
Govinda well enough
Govinda who
Govinda would

and kissed him
and knew

desire his worldly life
desired
desired to
desires
desiring
despair
desperate Siddhartha had drowned

# Writing through *Siddhartha*

everything always becomes
everything came back
everything can be learned
everything could be
Everything else
everything enter his mind
everything has
everything has existence
everything is
everything is Brahman
everything is coming
everything is easy
Everything is one-sided which can be thought
everything is perfect
everything only
everything shown
everything was

# *Acknowledgements*

*Writing through Siddhartha* is a found poem inspired by John Cage's experiments with James Joyce, namely *Writing through Finnegan's Wake* and *Writing for a Second Time through Finnegan's Wake.*

The text of Hermann Hesse's 1922 novel *Siddhartha* (the Project Gutenberg translation by Gunther Olesch et al.) has been processed by software called JanusNode, which ripped it into bits, sorted it alphabetically and distributed it to users for the purpose of Markov chaining experiments. I've taken selections from this JanusNode text and arranged them into a sequence.

Thank you Aaron Kent and Charlie Baylis.

WRITE THROUGH YOUR UNREST

www.ingramcontent.com/pod-product-compliance
Lightning Source LLC
Chambersburg PA
CBHW070803050426
42452CB00012B/2471